MIDDLE-EAST MEZZE

poems by
DAVID RADAVICH

Plain View Press
http://plainviewpress.net

3800 N. Lamar, 730-260
Austin, TX 78756

Copyright © 2011 David Radavich. All rights reserved under International and Pan-American Copyright Conventions. No part of this book may be reproduced or distributed in any form or by any means, or stored in a data base or retrieval system, without written permission from the author. All rights, including electronic, are reserved by the author and publisher.

ISBN: 978-1-935514-11-4
Library of Congress Number: 2010939943

Cover: A painting on wood by noted Syrian artist Elias Zayat. Reproduced with permission of Anne R. Zahlan.

Cover design by Susan Bright

Dedication

For those who suffered and who dream

Acknowledgments

The author would like to thank the editors and readers of the following publications in which individual poems from this collection have appeared: *Agora*, *Arabesques* (Algeria), *Damazine* (Syria), *Deus Loci*, *The New Verse News*, *North Central Review*, *Orbis* (UK), *Out of Line*, *The Pedestal*, *Poets Against the War*, *Prism Quarterly*, *The Scream*, *Voices in Wartime*, *Weyfarers* (UK), and *Writing the New South*. "Catacombs at Kom El Shogafa" and "Egyptian Time" appeared in *Knowing Stones: Poems of Exotic Places*, ed. Maureen Flannery (Burke, 2000). "Opening" appeared in *The Book of Hopes and Dreams*, ed. Dee Rimbaud (Bluechrome, UK, 2006). "Arabian Night," "Elixir," and "Dervish" appeared in my chapbook, *Canonicals: Love's Hours* (Finishing Line, 2009). Several poems in Section II appeared in *Literatures of War*, eds. Richard Pine and Eve Patten (Cambridge Scholars, UK, 2009). "Casualties" appeared in *Imagination & Place: Seasonings*, ed. Kelly Barth (Imagination & Place P, 2011).

CONTENTS

	On Finding a Tin	9
OPEN, SESAME		11
	Arabian Night	13
	Dervish	15
	Elixir	17
	Bitter Lemons	18
	Opening	19
	Arabesque	20
	Dance of Veils	21
	Carpet	23
IRAQ		25
	Curious War	27
	Forgetting	28
	On the Pillage of the Iraqi National Museum	29
	Echoes	31
	Airstrike	32
	Casualties	33
	Quagmire:	34
	Dispossessed	35
	Soldiers Home	36
	Dirge	37
	In the Mirror	38
	Gathering	40

PALESTINE   43

    Juxtapositions   45
    Judith and Me   47
    Chill   49
    West Bank   50
    Gaza   51
    Horror Show   52
    Gaza Guilt   53
    Diaspora   55
    Speaking   56
    Peace-Making   57
    Palestine   58

EGYPT   61

    Swimming Near El-Alamein   63
    Monastery at Wadi Natrun   65
    Catacombs at Kom El Shogafa   67
    Cavafy's House   69
    Egyptian Time   71
    Visiting an Alexandrine Mosque   72
    Along the Nile   73

Notes on the Poems   75
About the Author   77

Author's Note

For readers unfamiliar with Middle-Eastern cuisine, "mezze" is a smorgasbord of savory dishes (hummus, falafel, baba ghanoush, etc.) often served to groups of diners. This collection aims to provide a variety of tastes and perspectives of areas of the Middle East, ranging from the enchantments of myth and legend to the hard realities of oppression and war.

ON FINDING A TIN

Here is the desert:
Lasting sometimes
takes forever.

This could be
a circle for air,
the chalice that saves.

OPEN, SESAME

ARABIAN NIGHT

Once there was a man
with a wound
no one could see.

That could not be healed
by any medicine.

Sometimes
it would ooze with pus
and spill over every organ
with its poison.

He would writhe
like a snake and coil
into himself.

Or grab his groin
and growl like an animal.

Other times
he would open
his wound like a gift

and take this or
that jewel in his raw hands.

None of this could ever
be seen or heard.

His secret opened
and closed as the day-flower
in afternoon sun,

only the sun
did not open his secret
and could not heal.

Continued

One day a song
came over his ears
like a winter cap
and made him stop walking.

Music that would not
go away. Music

that somehow
wove pain into patterns
of skittering hues.

The hole
began to curl up
and speak its name and place.

The man learned
to accompany a chord
that was diminishing.

To move against sky.

Soon the song went away
into the wind,
and so did the wound.

The man was
left with his body
still dancing.

Some say this happened,
but who can know
if it is true?

DERVISH

Life is so needy
you can fill with a bucket,

take mop
and go swashing

what remains
along the floorboards

so crumbed
from the previous

ache I can
scarcely name.

Don't claim
you don't see what is

missing,
no sunshine is

capable, walls merely
echo our ghosts—

only time can
air out

the differences
like a Persian rug being

slapped in
all its intricate

Continued

threads patterning
the wind with

dancing
              emptiness

ELIXIR

How much
would you give

to open a magic tome
and find the remedy for what
you are suffering?

Ideally, two white pills,
a shot, even a suppository
supposing it works.

A face

that looks you
blue in the eye and says,

"It will get better."
"You are fundamentally sound."

So much within
the pages
of a book you imagine

having been able
to write

like an angel
whose wings touch
earth every thousand years.

BITTER LEMONS

Close up
the smell is almost
overwhelming

but restorative
in that way
of troubled history

when
icons fall

and bracing winds
blow through

without a
trace of compassion.

Pick it and hold
in your hand.

Sorrows are
meant to be borne

in their florid
colors, fragrance

piercing
even the night

of no torch

leading away.

OPENING

The mouth of
the hibiscus opens

exotic
as a promise,

self almost obscenely
in the world

against the garden fence
perhaps, or outside a library

whose books travel
farther than any beauty

we can reach without suffering,
shipwrecks: being borne

in a wind dried
without spring rain

dazzling even
trashcan and sidewalks,

tongue
pointing out

such bright and bold

possibilities

ARABESQUE

Lines interweave
like a flower

I can almost
smell

a presence above
and beyond dancing

in scorching sun
serene

as a pool
of limpid water

I step into
and never return

DANCE OF VEILS

Nothing is
ever truly lost.

It's just forlorn
as the sound
of jack-hammers
tearing apart

the real world.

I carry with me
many faces
long gone: coins

in my pocket
for the slot-machines
of life, songs

overheard
walking by an
exposed balcony

with a voice
that never forgets.

Sometimes the pain
comes back
like an orange

hanging ready
to drop

and to pick it
tastes bitter
in the mouth

Continued

but that rhythm
returns

and your face again
and all I've lost is myself
over and over

but somehow a body
moves forward

crab-like and sonorous
despite politicians

and the clamor
of public hypocrisy,

the dead seem to dance
around us in jest,

glad the earth
is under and beside,
never leaving.

Life too
is a memory.

CARPET

Help us to find
the exotic, the magical

where we can rise
out of our skin and fly almost

without wings, leaving
this tawdry world

in the dust.

Transport us now
to the Orient,

where everything
is dry and teeming with life.

Blazing sun
over earthen domes
and slim minarets

calls to prayer
facing low,

offers dates
and skewered meats,

lets us climb
on camels
and travel the vast

and always victorious sands.

Continued

But most of all
luxuriate in the red rugs

that seem to stretch everywhere—
on walls and store-fronts,

over sofas,
across canopies,

beneath
bended knees.

At every corner smells
claim us with frankincense

and musk, aromas
that conceal and invite.

No wonder Aladdin
forsook the real

and clung
to his fabled lamp:

dusk awakes phantoms,
desert seduces with mirage.

IRAQ

CURIOUS WAR

First of all, it's in our living room
like a close friend. With advertisements.

People smile as they are killing.
They admit it's inevitable.

The victims will be better off,
the weapons are sharper than ever.

Millions are turned by the ad campaign,
recalcitrants are so unpatriotic.

The pictures are indeed convincing:
It's a good story told by winners.

Our soldiers miss
their wives and boyfriends.

I could almost
vote for that, if I could vote.

And I wouldn't have
to feel anything.

That belongs to the freeze-framed,
the bombed, the orphaned,

blood that does not flow in our living rooms,
heads that don't explode on our carpets.

What a relief.

FORGETTING

War is not part of our memory.
It's something we do to others, to make
them memorize suffering which
we give to forget.

We do a lot of burying—only
now it's cremation: cleaner, simpler.

The ghosts of others
are not ghosts for us.

To live in the present,
to consume and satisfy
bodies, is to wash away time.

Only the rivers know
what we have killed, what
we have forgotten

hurrying against stones.

ON THE PILLAGE OF THE IRAQI NATIONAL MUSEUM

How easily we wipe out
heritage, whole civilizations.

I can't remember
what my hand touched

even an hour ago, let alone

what that lover, my best lover,
smelled like, kissed like
all those many years before.

We erase so many
life-lines of what is glorious
without thinking.

Illuminated manuscripts,
elaborate bowls, combs as golden
as the skin that screamed
against the hordes.

We all contribute
our Styrofoam detritus,
our failed human histories.

God bless the archivist,
the librarian who preserves
what we have forgotten

living in the dust
of monuments fallen

Continued

at the hands of purgers,
who wash off blood
in clean lavatories

with every convenience

every dry lie
our clock repeating arms—

so now we learn
what time will resurrect.

ECHOES

How can anyone sleep?

Fireflies turn the night over
like plows.

Stars have gone absent,
wanting justice.

Darkness reigns like a hawk,
clawing.

No wonder it's peaceful.

Only what is dead speaks.

Only the suffering listen
like children.

AIRSTRIKE

Follow
where it goes

where it ends up
beyond

the wings
in the wind turning

blistering
speed

screaming
eyes

taking hope
hostage

into the cracked
center

that justifies
everything

CASUALTIES

Leaves spiral
in their camouflage,

each one
a friend falling

in spring
against everything

I have known
of seasons,

buds banished
in discovery

by the old
who stand barren

as scarecrows,
rooted

too stiff and
empty of essence—

this storm
now ransacking youth

tearing out
hair

of the angels

QUAGMIRE:

where bodies sink
without trying

an alien force no one knows
or should have known

struggling only
makes everything worse

eyes see now darker
than anyone had planned

just beyond reach
the hand that might rescue

history sinking
of its own mad weight

this emptiness
now covering itself

in the dry sun
in the dry and dusty sun

DISPOSSESSED

What do we not talk about?

What do we not say,
now that every dark night
can be electrified,
every moon traveled to
flagged
and revisited,

every bomb blows white as sun
what most we feared,
dispossessed
as if it had never seen
into our fear and called forth
our furious
dance of righteousness—

What can we not say,
now that we're so cornered
with ourselves,
so sure of firm footing

that our shoes miss
the path that was waiting,
eyes flutter believing
all shadows have been lost—

while in the dark forest
words run from us

with fear in their eyes
like refugees

SOLDIERS HOME

That is not a flag
hiding a corpse.

That is not a man
who failed to live out
his span.

That is not
a war

but a performance
of return.

The family, the public
need not witness
the arrival.

The plane disgorges
like a giant fish.

The box is carried out
by uniforms.

Trumpets help
to silence the sun.

This is not
a poem about war.

You do not
hear any grief.

You do not read
any shame.

DIRGE

In a time of war

An ear to the ground
measures dust.

The wind
catches its breath

among trees.

Where does it stop
when face

falls into itself
like a burst balloon?

Tatters
of a colored

flag at the end
of a lance, a dance

of no design.

Who can reckon
the rhythm?

Who can utter
the words?

IN THE MIRROR

Who knows the real Iraq?

Before the
all-consuming mirage

of shock and awe

where Adam
and Eve walked
unself-consciously,

gardens hanged
their brilliant blossoms,

the alphabet
was first
scratched down
from ibises' tiny feet.

Not to mention
palaces with blue walls,
gold lions and bulls,

Ishtar's grand colonnade
nor the great bazaars

or insistent
minarets of Islamic
learning, intricate carvings
and drapes,

Qurans that whisper
their sacred dust
to centuries.

Who knows the real Iraq

better than the stones
that lie scattered

as human eyes

seeing walls
groveling

the sun
as slave-master

drives away
all love.

GATHERING

In honor of Mahmoud Darwish

The one with the tin cup
stands at the podium
reading from the masters.

What is it they all want
from mere scratches on a page

that nonetheless
make faces weep or guffaw

and the air thick
with a lived sharing

and music
of a kind that sometimes
repeats and sometimes sounds
like a gong or a whizz

beside birds or water
or even fire

and ears gather
like elders around their stones
at the center of a circle

whose periphery narrows
with ghosts and chants

and an old truck drives through
delivering long-delayed
necessities

that disaster-ridden
hands reach for

after the storm has left
and the sun shines through

with its gold eye

thinking of renewal

PALESTINE

JUXTAPOSITIONS

A man enters a mosque
at Friday prayers

Israeli settler

opens fire with automatic death,
gutters more than forty

worshipping Allah

Blood shot on sacred
rugs, red on red

each head bowed forward

forever

live snapping beads
collapsing on their string

wailing at the wall

forever

We see before us the films
gaunt and horrible

Nazi Germany

clutching the last wall
the rings, brick by ashen brick

Continued

sinking, gasping
before us

ghost-blackened face

How they meet

Man of the holocaust ovens
Man in the mosque at
Friday prayers

JUDITH AND ME

I've never written about this,
so please forgive me.

It's a bit embarrassing—
woman cutting off a man's head
after he's drunk

and lustful,
carrying it around
in a basket, bright testicle—

not a fit story
for company. I always

cringe
at her cleverness.

The perfect ruse against
manhood

that knows its power
beyond keeping.

Beautify yourself—
silk and jewels and perfume—

and enter
that war-driven territory

where love is never
known

and all enemies
are equal.

Continued

Cut it off. Hold it high.
The brain no longer

thinks,
eyes peer out

at night and falling.

I've been taken like that
and never knew

the woman
who served me.

CHILL

Night settles over us
as a crisp wind in Jerusalem.

The old apse
has flowered dust,

is empty now, with no
congregation.

Cold rakes through its sacred tines.

There's no escaping
walls, oppression, altitude
of difference:

No god

(so far as I know)
can sleep with another;

none's content to be slave.

Wherefore the darkness carries
a knife in its white sleeve.

WEST BANK

Nothing quite grips
the throat like a scythe

cutting across
all sound—

injustice of history,
pillage, denial of rights,

a girl burned
a boy bayoneted

for an ideology
that lives still buried

in its own blood.

All this I merely imagine
from bull-dozed

windows that
close out the sun

like God
during the Flood.

GAZA

The terrorist aggressors
have no homes, no food, no hospitals.

The victims have warplanes
and bombs, tanks and body armor.

The terrorists bury
their dead.

The victims fly over
and hold press conferences.

The terrorists seek
martyrdom through God.

The victims seek
territory with no Other.

The terrorists have elected
the wrong leaders.

The victims won't tolerate
the choices of terrorists.

Now they meet
as dark brothers.

Rubble
and aggrieved.

One day they will home
in the same earth.

HORROR SHOW

On the TV

it is hard to tell
victims from survivors.

They melt like dust,
like shadows.

Nobody can blame *us*
who live safe in our snug houses.

Only the bombs are
at fault,

only the planes
dropping like vultures

on sand,
on monuments.

We merely watch
without eyes

from our
warm bleachers.

GAZA GUILT

I confess: I didn't really see
the grief-stricken girl
by the seashore.

I didn't know her suffering.
I've only seen pictures.

That's why it
didn't seem real.

But I felt for her
genuine pain.

And images came
to me—

unlocking their shapes,
their unforgettable
colors.

You will please
forgive me.

Honesty is best.

Even dull honesty
with no ripped-off heads
bloody and toy-like

that only have
been imagined by

the privileged
who in their silence

Continued

collude
and oppress.

I am safe and warm.
I have food. And money.
I don't see bodies

torn by war
for breakfast.

The blind can
never do justice.

DIASPORA

Someone
took our home,
our business

for a crime
committed a continent,
a war away—

sun stolen sky—

and now
we are homeless
forever,

the stones
that spoke our names
have gone silent,

obedient

to history
and power
and forgetting.

O let the wandering
remember

remember

SPEAKING

A word pours forth
from a child

with a past,
consciousness, a future

I even see
a shadow cast

against the wall, sun
or no sun

and a grave
waiting

and in-between
stars and blackest night

bombs
leveling a house

air aching
upward

making the sound
of speaking

bald
as a flower

PEACE-MAKING

It's not so hard
as it sounds—

arm around a shoulder,
kiss, or maybe

just a
few words.

Thank you.
I'm sorry.

On the battlefield
begin at the beginning:
gratitude.

Daffodils open
from bitter seeds

sought
by raw wings
over screaming nests.

You, too,
can fly above

anger, take away
your hand from the fire.

Yours is the face
that must turn

to the sun.

PALESTINE

For Taha Muhammad Ali

I don't know which way
the wind blows.

Whether history
will be able to recover

its haphazard blooms
or fields greening casually
under a warring sun.

So much blood
has been
spilled into rivers—

how can it be swept
colorless into the seas?

Our former homes
have been demolished,

stones for us
are but memories
we collect like coins.

All I have is
my mind

and that is fading
as the scent
of persimmons.

Even my bones
do not keep a good house
but ache in ceaseless
going and going.

Somehow the soil
must not blow away
but learn
to breathe again

so the souls
who walked here once

can be reborn.

EGYPT

SWIMMING NEAR EL-ALAMEIN

This bluest green water
eyes have ever seen, shimmering
against white sand

soft as seashells melted
to carpets of pearl—

massages each toe,
each leg, each strand of hair.

No time is enough
to linger

in this world

no body
too old, too worn,
too ulcerous.

These arms spread wide,
these eyes, sun takes its bow,

voices of strangers,
children, sudden friends
laugh

each wave home

too fast

I see your face
calling with a towel,

Continued

welcome, offer of cigarettes,
and the best day's end

hosting the return

we don't want
we never want

what the world calls us to

dark labyrinths
of fate

Our pain has flown,
let it stay on the wing:

wide over the jeweling sea

its shield of gold

MONASTERY AT WADI NATRUN

How to make sense
of need?—

Christians in a Muslim
land, disciples of St. Mark,

the Alexandrine
visitor,

these herds of camels
loping, sand pastures, wind-
blown shrubs and

then
these crosses,
multiplying in rows

as necklaces,

breast upon sanded breast
with slitted eyes,

dry hollow passages

through time

This is the desert
beyond words.

God rounded to chapels
in punishing sun,

wind flailing
the brazen flame trees

Continued

and this horde
of humans

touching the sacred
relic, summoning strength

from bone necessity

a life in sand

that stays and stays

The cleric robes
hang loosely, simply
in the heat, move graciously

as naked feet begin

to pray.

CATACOMBS AT KOM EL SHOGAFA

Down and down
this cylinder winds,

necropolis of cultures

into the earth,

Pharaonic, Ptolemaic,
Roman images superimposed,

wearing each other's
inscriptions,
faces, clothing—

one must be safe
about the underworld,

respect all gods

adorn all sarcophagi

remember where life goes
and stays

We bend our necks,
crane and weasel our way
along this deepest

memory

dialogue of history,
human ingenuity

Continued

to face
the other life

in rock, with swords
and sheaves

May the journey
be peaceful, fulfilling:

the gods of time

safely

engraved

beside us

CAVAFY'S HOUSE

The face, I think.

Lingers from a high house
above this balcony

overlooking

the laundry
of everyday life.

Ignorant of the words
that emanated

from this
marbled face

amid the tattered books
of a life, a being

in rooms
in ancient songs,

these multitudes
come and go

in their daily worn bodies

like rhyming ghosts

A beggar asks
a fee,

stands to profit
the memory of a poet

Continued

who lived
who lives

sequestered

beyond a street
that offers cameras,
leather, jewels, the rugs

of nomads,

who traveled farther
than all these

naming

heroes in air.

EGYPTIAN TIME

Impossible! A giant horse
dancing through the hotel lobby
with a brass band, throwing out coins.

The bride comes after
her flowered accomplices,
and then the groom, a bit red-faced,
with taunting friends screaming
to join, to join, to sing,
to dance, to play.

Tired and not young,
heavy with witnessing, late
beyond years—

of course we do.

Some with cameras,
some with their own red feet,
the trinkets aside,
real coins, gaped smiles,

and the abandon
of a horse on four human legs
leaping beyond all check-out counters,
porters, maitre d's, sofas,
chairs, beyond tourist and native,
Arab, Christian, Muslim,
brown or red, tired or young—

to follow a music so raucous
and riveting, so wed of all catching life
we cannot deny the trumpets,
pretend, unjoin, or fail to snake along,
chanting the love-night on.

VISITING AN ALEXANDRINE MOSQUE

We leave our shoes,
tiptoe over rugs in silence,
wife among women,
myself among reclining
men who read or sleep or
think or merely be.

It's cavernous, this dome,
and fully carved, the chandelier
must weigh some tons.

Some thousand marvels
yet this ease, this hanging
around in time

eye of the city
calm
unblinking

a faceted jewel

to circumflect inside

It's hard to put on
shoes again

this treading to busy streets,
vendors and vended,

horns shrieking

this calm to veiling
memory

ALONG THE NILE

This could be the Mississippi,
the Ohio, the Missouri,

but the mind
knows better—

palm trees, mansions
on either side, gleaming
mosque at the crook
of the current,

Cleopatra somewhere
glittering on her barge—

it's a lesson in
recognition and return.

We have been
in this small wooden
hand-hewn skiff

puttering by ourselves

since childhood,

collecting shells
at the mouth
where waves right-angle
before our eyes

lunching under
grass-roofed tables

Continued

patrolling along
the limestone ramparts—

We have been
crafting these waters
for years,

papyrus growing
and being harvested

orange trees and
frangipani

workmen painting
their great wood boats—

We know in a wind
where we are.

Notes on the Poems

"Arabian Night."

Several poems in this first section refer to the famous mediaeval work popularly known as *The Thousand and One Arabian Nights*. This remarkable sequence of inter-locking stories is told by Scheherazade, beautiful young wife to the King. At the outset, the King is disaffected and cruel, but through the magic of her story-telling, he eventually becomes healed. The poems here also suggest the contemporary Arab world's need/desire for healing and renewal.

"Soldiers Home."

This poem was written in response to the policy of U.S. President George W. Bush prohibiting any pictures of arriving coffins from the war in Iraq.

"Judith and Me."

The speaker of this poem is the Assyrian general Holofernes, whose seduction and subsequent beheading by the Jewish title character is recounted in the Apocryphal Book of Judith.

"Swimming near El-Alamein."

This famous World War II battle site is marked by a museum and three international cemeteries.

ABOUT THE AUTHOR

David Radavich is the author of *Slain Species* (Court Poetry, London), *By the Way* (Buttonwood, 1998), and *Greatest Hits* (Pudding House, 2000). His plays have been performed across the U.S., including six Off-Off-Broadway productions. *Fragments of the Third Planet* received its European premiere in 2000 in Germany. *America Bound: An Epic for Our Time* (Plain View Press, 2007) narrates American history from World War II to the present. *Canonicals* (Finishing Line, 2009) is an anatomy of "love's hours." Radavich has read his work in a variety of locations, including Canada, England, Egypt, Germany, Greece, and Iceland. He lives in Charlotte, North Carolina.

www.ingramcontent.com/pod-product-compliance
Lightning Source LLC
Chambersburg PA
CBHW052115070526
44584CB00017B/2490